Comforting Scents

A Personal Aromatherapy Journal

Comforting Scents

A Personal Aromatherapy Journal

Valerie Gennari Cooksley

PRENTICE HALL PRESS

Library of Congress Cataloging-in-Publication Data

Cooksley, Valerie Gennari.
     Comforting scents / by Valerie Gennari Cooksley.
        p. cm.
     ISBN 0-7352-0002-5
     1. Aromatherapy. I. Title.
RM666.A68C663   1998
615'.321—dc21   97-32868
                                                             CIP

Printed in the United States of America

10 9 8 7 6 5 4 3 2 1

ISBN   0-7352-0002-5

PRENTICE HALL PRESS
Paramus, NJ 07652

A Simon & Schuster Company

On the World Wide Web at http://www.phdirect.com

Prentice Hall International (UK) Limited, *London*
Prentice Hall of Australia Pty. Limited, *Sydney*
Prentice Hall Canada, Inc., *Toronto*
Prentice Hall Hispanoamericana, S.A., *Mexico*
Prentice Hall of India Private Limited, *New Delhi*
Prentice Hall of Japan, Inc., *Tokyo*
Simon & Schuster Asia Pte. Ltd., *Singapore*
Editora Prentice Hall do Brasil, Ltda., *Rio de Janeiro*

Dedication

In Memory of my Father

Angelo Victor Gennari (May 30, 1922–May 21, 1997)

*A wise, resourceful and humble man
whose soulful journey of spirit was in harmony with nature.
He took pleasure in planting, growing and harvesting
all ten acres of his gardens in New England—
vegetables, berries, herbs and flowers.
His way of life instilled a love of nature in me
a foundation which will continue to bear fruit
long after his departure from this earthly landscape.
His strength, perseverance, and faith
will live on through generation to generation,
through his children, grandchildren, and great grandchildren
and all who were blessed to have known him.*

Preface

There is nature in all things.
Aromatic flowers, fruits and seeds keep their essences
in different manners,
and release their lovely scents when the time is right.
We too are distinctive in displaying our uniqueness,
innermost feelings and dreams.
Some may express and emanate their beauty freely and openly,
like a flower in full bloom. Others are more guarded, storing their
inner strength deep within their roots of being,
like the heavier scents born of heartwood, resins and roots.
Every form of expression is perfect...individualized and personal.
It is this fragrant celebration of life
manifested in the flowering and herbaceous botanicals,
aromatic grasses, heartwood and fruits that surround us
that create rejuvenating salve and comforting scents
for our health and pleasure.

VALERIE GENNARI COOKSLEY

Introduction

Comforting scents is not a new concept. People from every major culture have employed aromatics for health, pleasure and ceremonial representation. Journal writing too is nothing new. However, the union of both is a refreshing notion to tap into hidden reservoirs of past experiences and new alike.

Over the years I have collected nature-inspired pieces of poetry, quotes and proverbs that were meaningful to me. I share this redolent wisdom with you in the pages to come along with some of my own personal thoughts. I have reveled in nature in many forms, from gardening, studying botanical medicine and aromatherapy, to taking up botanical illustration and photographing the beauty of the landscape. I was raised as a child to appreciate nature and learned through experiences of living on a farm, caring for animals and tending acres of herb, vegetable and hay fields.

I thank my parents for this upbringing, especially my father, for his influence in instilling in me a deep connection with all living things. Sorrowfully, I lost my father very recently. The week upon returning to my home in Washington State I received a phone call from my publishing editor. He asked for my thoughts on writing an aromatherapy journal-type book. Although in the midst of grief and feelings of loss, I decided to write the book you are holding, seeing it not simply as a coincidence, but as an opportune and meaningful fruition of divine intercession. I have dedicated it lovingly to the memory of my father and hope that it brings comfort to others in times of loss, sorrow and feelings of isolation.

Comforting Scents is also a means for celebration, self exploration and appreciation of nature and all its fragrant pleasures. It contains a unique bouquet of recipes, remedies and thoughtful suggestions for body, mind and spirit. You are invited to experiment, experience, and to pen your own aromatic creations on the unfilled pages, keeping your ideas of gardening, flower gathering and personal aromatherapy recipes at hand. Use this journal as a tool for reflection, self discovery and be open to new sensory experiences. An array of botanicals displayed in bloom, bearing fruit and seed, are strewn over the blank pages for you to imprint your thoughts, feelings, memories and dreams as well. Just as the scents and visual beauty of nature are very real—so are your innermost visions and cerebrations.

The seeds are planted here for you. Read. Contemplate. Explore. My heartfelt hope is for you to experience this connection through perusing Comforting Scents and embrace life fully, finding joy in the abundant fragrances and self introspection. Throughout the journal I have included aromatic introductions to inspirit the imagination and acquaint you with the scented botanical, its essence and the health-giving benefits of their precious essential oils. Walk in life with expectancy to see, smell and taste the abundant gifts our Creator has bestowed upon this earth. Be grateful, take pleasure in and protect these botanicals so that future generations will also delight in their emanation. Reflect and put forth your flowers.

Aromatically Yours,

Valerie Gennari Cooksley
September 1997

Opening the following pages is likened to a flower unfolding ...
opening of spirit,
surrendering its fragrance
in discovery of self.

VALERIE GENNARI COOKSLEY

Jasmine

Jasminum grandiflorum, J. officinale

asmine is well known for having powerful effects on the metaphysical level as well as for possessing male and female (yin and yang) characteristics. Try a drop or two in an aroma lamp to create a sacred space for meditation, or mix in jojoba oil for a perfumed anointment. Alternatively, you may want to scent your favorite prayer beads or amulet with this exalting fragrance.

Known as Common White Jasmine, it is one of over 150 species, which were derived from the Persian "Yasmin", native to Northern India and Persia. Intensely fragrant after dusk, the white or yellow tubular star-shaped flowers with dark green leaves grow on hardy ligneous climbing vines. The delicate flowers produce minute amounts of essential oil and must be solvent-extracted to yield an absolute which is viscous and orange-brown in color. The exotic fragrance is heavy-floral, sweet and rich with a tea-like background note. Well known for its aphrodisiac, euphoric and antidepressant character, Jasmine oil is also a pain-relieving, anti-inflammatory and antiseptic balm for physical ailments, such as aging skin, childbirth analgesia and hormone balancing support.

"… the vines and blossoms have given faith their fragrance."

SONG OF SOLOMON 2 : 13

*Cultivate your inner garden
by looking to words
rooted in nature
to nourish the soul
and refresh the spirit.*

VALERIE GENNARI COOKSLEY

Hyssop

Hyssopus officinalis

Known since ancient times as a strewing herb to aid in purifying environments, Hyssop means "holy herb" in Greek "azob" as it was used to clean sacred places as well. A Mediterranean evergreen herbaceous shrub, it has woody stems and lance-shaped leaves that put forth purple-blue flowers. A clear to pale yellow-green essential oil is steam-distilled from the flowers and leaves producing a fresh, herbal, spicy-sweet aroma with a light camphoraceous top note. An excellent mucolytic and antiseptic, Hyssop is most often incorporated in respiratory blends for chest colds, sore throats, sinus congestion, bronchitis and asthma conditions. It encourages alertness and mental clarity and aids in regulating both the circulatory and nervous systems.

Hyssop can be easily used in a steam inhalation for respiratory ailments by placing two to three drops in a bowl of hot water. For chronic or recurring infections try using several drops of Hyssop in a cool water humidifier for a continuous restorative treatment.

*"But flowers distilled
though they with winter meet,
Lose but their show;
their substance still lives sweet."*

WILLIAM SHAKESPEARE

"In search of my mother's garden I found my own."

ALICE WALKER

$\mathcal{Y}$ou may already have some of these deliciously fragrant and tasteful herbs and flowers growing in your garden; however, if they are not included as of yet you will want to add them for their pleasant infusion bouquet. Use these botanicals fresh from the garden to prepare a tisane or dry them carefully and store in labeled glass jars. To make a hot infusion with a single herb or combination, place two to three teaspoons in a cup of near-boiling water and steep for five minutes. Strain, sweeten if desired and enjoy.

A Collection of Herbs for the Tea Garden

Anise (Pimpenelaa anisum), Chamomile (Matricaria recutita), Catnip (Nepeta cataria), Hyssop (Hyssopus officinalis), Lemonbalm (Melissa officinalis), Lemon Verbena (Aloysia triphylla), Pineapple Sage (Salvia elegans) and all mints, roses, scented basils, lavenders and scented geraniums.

*"Be glad of life
because it gives you the chance
to love and to work and to play
and to look up at the stars."*

HENRY VAN DYKE

Sweet Breath Seed Mix

1 part Anise Seed
1 part Fennel Seed
1 part Caraway Seed

*I*n many Eastern and European countries, seeds of specific plants were chewed following a meal to aid in digestion and freshen the breath. It is the essential oils inherent in the seeds that make them effective. Make the recipe above and store in a decorative jar for at home and tuck some in your purse or office drawer.

"Your seeds shall live in my body,
and your buds of your tomorrow shall blossom in my heart,
And your fragrance shall be my breath,
And together we shall rejoice through all the seasons."

KAHLIL GIBRAN

Petitgrain

Citrus aurantium, C. bigardia

*T*raditionally the small unripe green fruits of the Bitter Orange tree were used to extract the oil, giving its name "petit grain" or little grain. However, today the leaves and twigs of the Orange tree are steam distilled to produce the essential oil of Petitgrain. The oil is pale yellow to light amber in color and has a fresh, floral-citrus and bitter-sweet bouquet with green overtones. Petitgrain oil possesses antiseptic, tonic and antispasmodic properties. This refreshing oil is slightly cooling and uplifting and is an aid to depressive and nervous states.

Try a drop or two on a tissue to inhale, or place a few drops on a fan to disperse the clean renewing essence throughout a room. This essential oil can be easily incorporated into the workplace as it is a well-liked and tonifying scent.

*"Nature teaches me more than she preaches.
There are no sermons in stones.
It is easier to get a spark out of a stone than a moral."*

JOHN BURROUGHS

*H*ere are some suggestions that encourage solace-in-nature—from fun and frolic to restful pleasures. Create your personal stress-relief "order of the day." If you are a workaholic-type, write the activity in your day timer and schedule it in. Self-care should be a priority—so make it one and have fun!

Nature's Stress Reducers

Skip rocks on a lake—keep a journal—take a walk with a friend—feed the ducks

Simplify your life—go kite flying on a windy day—listen to a brook or waterfall

take a long, warm, aromatic bath—visit a botanical garden or park—look at the stars

eat by candlelight—pet a dog or cat—listen to the ocean in a shell—grow a garden

brew your favorite herb tea—go bird watching—climb a tree—build a sand castle

go on a picnic—sit under a tree and daydream …

"Come forth into the light of things.
Let Nature be your teacher."

WILLIAM WORDSWORTH

"I go to Nature to be soothed,
and healed,
and to have my senses
put in tune once more."

JOHN BURROUGHS

"For what is prayer but the expansion of yourself
into the living ether? And it is for your comfort
to pour your darkness into space, it is also for your delight
to pour forth the dawning of your heart."

KAHLIL GIBRAN

"My heart is tuned to the quietness that
the stillness of nature inspires."

HAZRAT INAYAT KHAN

Comforting poetry, comforting scents …

*T*he key ingredient in this synergistic blend is the tranquilizing Frankincense—the most highly esteemed incense known to man. Peace and Love lends quiet contentment to the end of a troubled day, allaying fears and worries with its redolent incense.

Peace and Love

a meditation synergy

18 drops Frankincense essential oil
10 drops Lavender essential oil
10 drops Sandalwood (or Myrrh) essential oil
5 drops Cedarwood essential oil
5 drops Ylang-ylang essential oil

*M*ix the above essential oils in an amber glass bottle and label. Used in the pure form, a few drops can be placed in an aroma lamp or potpourri burner for inhalation. Diluted in vegetable oil, this recipe can be added to two ounces of sweet almond or olive oil and one teaspoon of jojoba oil to make an anointment oil.

Frankincense

Boswellia carterii

*A*lso named Olibanum or Oil of Lebanon, because this small tree is native to the Red Sea region. Since ancient times Frankincense has been highly regarded as an incense and dates back to 2,800 B.C. In Medieval French "franc" means pure and abundant and refers to the oleo-resin collected from this "incense" tree with pinnate leaves and pale pink flowers. Cuts in the bark allow the milky fluid to become exposed to the air where it hardens into amber-colored tears in about three months time. These tears are steam-distilled to produce a clear to pale yellow spice-like woody fragrance oil with a rich balsamic undertone. This oil improves with age and is used traditionally in a wide variety of health conditions such as for aged skin, wounds, ulcers; in addition, it is a stress-reducer, sedative and meditation essence.

Incense was the earliest use of aromatic plants. The word "perfume" comes from the Latin derivation "per fumum" meaning "through smoke." The ancients used nature's fragrant gifts as "burnt offerings" to communicate with God by burning special woods, resins, herbs and flowers, while they recited verses and petitions. They believed the smoke carried the prayers up to the heavens.

Food nourishes the body,
but flowers heal the soul.

OLD PROVERB

Ginger Honey

A healthful nectar

This aromatic honey can be used as a digestive aid, cold remedy or just an enjoyable sweetener.

1 1/2 cups raw honey
2 inch piece fresh ginger root, thinly sliced
1–2 teaspoons dried ground ginger (optional)

Heat honey over low setting. Add sliced ginger and heat gently, taking care not to boil. Taste test in 15 to 20 minutes. It should be flavorful and the ginger pieces almost dry. The essential oil from the root is being extracted out into the honey. Strain with a slotted spoon. Store in a clean glass jar and label. If you own a dehydrator, save the ginger slices and sprinkle with sugar and dry to make ginger candy.

Ginger

Zinziber officinalis

*J*amaican Ginger, as it is commonly named, has been used as a spice and folk remedy for thousands of years. A perennial native of South Asia and Africa, this long narrow plant with reed-like leaves produces white and yellow blooms from a center shoot. The roots, or tuberous rhizomes, are used to produce the distilled stimulating aromatic oil. A pale yellow-amber liquid with a warm balsamic, slightly lemon-peppery overtone is known as an analgesic, tonic and carminative. Traditional uses include aid in muscular pain, encouraging circulation and aiding memory.

Try a drop or two of Ginger essential oil in your favorite unscented natural hand cream to alleviate the aches and pains of arthritic joints and stiff fingers. Alternatively, you can add two to four drops to one-quarter cup of sea salt and one-quarter cup of Epsom salts and pour into a basin of warm water to soak your hands or cold feet. This is a warming and invigorating bath soak to release muscle tightness and provide gentle pain relief.

Lavender, Roses, Lilacs, Peonies, Phlox, Scented Geraniums, Heliotrope, Sweet Peas, Osmanthus, Daphne, Lilies, Iris germanica, Lily of the Valley, Muscari, hardy Jasmines, Narcissus, Rosemary, Basil, Mints of all kinds and Thyme. Plant these perfume-bearers close to paths, sitting areas and doorways to get the most from their delightful efflorescence.

"Love ... is like a beautiful flower
which I may not touch, but whose fragrance
makes the garden a place of delight just the same."

HELEN KELLER

Lemon

Citrus limonum, C. medica

Over 40 cultivated varieties of Lemon are now grown, but were originally native to Asia and have become naturalized in the Mediterranean region as well as in California and Florida, USA. The name was derived from the Arabic "Limun" and has been traditionally used as a general antiseptic, as well as an English seaman's remedy for scurvy. It grows on a small thorny evergreen tree that grows a little over 15 feet tall and produces small white fragrant flowers and bright yellow fruit. The fruit peels are cold-expressed to yield a pale yellow-green oil with a fresh, clean sharp aroma that is cooling, uplifting and bright. Noted most for its antibacterial and immune enhancing properties, Lemon essential oil also promotes circulation, aids concentration and is an excellent remedy for general debility.

Drop a small amount of Lemon essential oil on your writing paper or note-pad to keep you alert and focused during the day at work. In the home, place a few drops of this purifying and invigorating essential oil on the vacuum cleaner bag, the side of the toilet paper roll; add it to unscented cleaners or mix into baking soda to create a carpet freshener that can be vacuumed up to absorb undesirable odors.

*"The best and most beautiful things in the world
cannot be seen or even touched.
They must be felt with the heart."*

Fragrant Repose

A deep relaxation synergy

6 parts Lavender essential oil
2 parts Marjoram essential oil
1 part Mandarin essential oil

Use an electric aromatherapy diffuser for subtle environmental dispersion. These specially designed machines do not involve heat to make the essences airborne, therefore optimizing their therapeutic benefits for mood enhancement and natural air purification.

Alternatively, place a few drops in an aroma lamp or on a tissue.

Sweet Marjoram

Origanum marjorana, Marjorana hortensis

*A*lso named Knotted Marjoram, this culinary herb was popular among the ancient Greeks as a medicinal as well as a token of good fortune. In Latin "Marjor" means great and attributed to long life, whereas the Greek meaning of "orosganos" is joy of the mountain. Native to Egypt, the Mediterranean and North Africa, this tender herbaceous perennial has aromatic green-grey ovate leaves with tiny white or pale purple flowers which grow in clusters or "knots." The oil is distilled from the dried flowering herb and displays a pale yellow to light amber color. Marjoram's spicy aroma is warmly herbal, woody and slightly camphoraceous. Traditionally known for promoting good health on many levels, it is especially beneficial for the circulatory and nervous systems. It aids regulation of mental/nervous imbalances, anxiety, stress, grief, sorrow, heart palpitations and hypertension.

A single drop of Marjoram essential oil on a pillowcase or pajama collar can help relieve insomnia due to mental stress and emotional upheaval. It provides a restful and peaceful essence that reportedly stimulates the brain to produce and release serotonin, the body's natural hormone that promotes relaxation.

*"Happiness is not a state to arrive at,
but a manner of traveling."*

MARGARET LEE RUNBECK

Ultimately it is not one particular thing or activity that will bring you long-lasting happiness. Rather, it is the little things on a regular basis that are more apt to bring one joy, inner peace and contentment. Start a positive self-nurturing routine of taking an aromatic bath more frequently, perhaps once per week or more, for pleasure, affirmation and health.

Botanical Bath

An indulgent bath to replenish and nourish the entire body

1/4 cup aloe vera gel or juice
1/4 cup milk or cream
2 Tablespoons honey
2 Tablespoons baking soda
1/4 cup sea salt
8 drops Lavender essential oil
2 drops Clary Sage essential oil
1 Tablespoon powdered spirulina seaweed
or whole seaweed frond (optional)

Mix in a 2 cup measuring cup. Add to warm-hot bath after it has been drawn. Soak quietly or listen to your favorite nature-inspired music. Wrap yourself in a thick all-cotton bathrobe and snuggle up in bed or a comfy lounge chair and write in your journal.

Clary Sage

Salvia sclarea

*C*lary is derived from the Latin "clarus" which means "clear." The seeds from this three-foot European native plant were once used in the Middle Ages to improve eyesight. Also known as Muscatel Sage, this herbaceous plant's heart-shaped leaves were used to flavor German wines. The small blue flowers and leaves are steam-distilled to produce a clear to pale yellowish-green essential oil. The balancing effects of this warm, nutty-herbal odoriferous liquid are best reflected in women. Used traditionally for PMS symptoms, regulating menses and supporting childbirth, it provides a pleasing euphoric essence supportive in depressed states, mental and physical imbalances, and heightens a feeling of well being. Also antiseptic in nature, it is used widely for sore throat infections and skin care.

Especially helpful during stressful periods and hormonal imbalances, Clary sage essential oil is best inhaled to directly stimulate the thalamus, the portion of the brain that produces enkephalins, or the "feel good" hormone that creates a state of euphoria. Try two to four drops in your unscented body lotion (enough for one application) or a few drops in the bath as given in the recipe on the previous page.

"If instead of a gem, or even a flower,
we should cast the gift of a loving thought
into the heart of a friend,
that would be giving as the angels give."

GEORGE MACDONALD

1 cup Distilled water or Rose Floral Water
1 cup Honey
1 cup firmly packed red or pink Rose petals
1 Tablespoon beet juice (optional for additional color)

*A*dd water and rose petals to a blender and thoroughly blend. Pour into a heavy sauce pan and bring to a boil. Cover and reduce heat and simmer for five minutes. Strain through a fine tea strainer and bottle.

Delicious Ideas:

*D*ivine on vanilla ice cream garnished with fresh clean rose petals, or add a few teaspoons in sparkling mineral water and serve with ice cubes frozen with rose petals inside for a delightful drink.

Rose

Rosa damascena

*T*here are many different subspecies of Rose, believed to be native to Northern Persia, but cultivated worldwide today. Also known as Damask or Bulgarian Rose, this small deciduous shrub has thorny stems, whitish-green hairy leaves and large deep pink fragrant flowers bearing thirty-six petals. Rose otto or Attar of Rose is the essential oil produced by steam distillation of the fresh flowers, yielding approximately one pound of oil to every 8–10,000 pounds of petals. Rose otto is colorless to pale yellow with a tint of green and is semi-solid at cool temperature. Rose absolute is yellow-orange and viscous as it is solvent-extracted and is used for perfume purposes. The opulent aroma of pure rose oil is deeply rich, sweet-floral with a hint of vanilla-honey undertone. Highly prized as a powerful antidepressant and supremely feminine, this soothing and beautiful essence is effective in rejuvenating skincare, emotional imbalance and is a general neuro-tonic.

Due to its high cost, use this precious essential oil sparingly by holding a few drops in a perfume pendant, and inhale occasionally when support and encouragement are needed. Attar of Rose is worth every penny for "gladdening the heart." Truly a burst into bloom essence.

"Though we travel the world over to find the beautiful,
we must carry it within us,
or we find it not."

Floral essences that inspirit an appreciation of Beauty and Love:

Bulgarian Rose (Rosa damascena),
Jasmine (Jasminum grandiflorum, J. officinale),
Neroli (Citrus aurantium, flos) and
Ylang-ylang (Canaga odorata).

$\mathcal{S}$ingle notes of the springtime flower essences above, or a combination of them, will create a floral bouquet sure to delight and increase your awareness of all things beautiful. A simple perfume formulation may have astounding effects! Try two tablespoons of jojoba oil with one to four drops (total) of your favorite essential oil or absolute. Store in a dark glass perfume bottle and apply to nape of neck and pulse points with a light touch.

"There is a landscape larger than the one you see."

AUTHOR UNKNOWN

Ylang-Ylang

Canaga odorata

Known in tropical Asia, where it is native, as the Flower of Flowers, Poor Man's Jasmine or Perfume Tree. Indonesian villagers customarily pick these arousing blossoms and place them on the beds of newlyweds. A 100-foot tree with arching branches and large ovate glossy leaves, its abundant fragrant yellow green-tinged flowers are steam-distilled into four grades of essential oil. The first distillate is considered the finest and displays a pale yellow color and is called Ylang-ylang extra. The aroma of this oil is heavy, sweetly exotic and floral with a creamy-almond balsamic undertone. Successive distillates will produce less top note characteristics. A warming and intoxicating floral essence that possesses euphoric, aphrodisiac and antidepressant qualities, it is known to benefit emotional coldness, nervous tension, fear and shock. Its attributes relieve hypertension and rapid heart beat. It is a uterine tonic and is also used in skin and hair preparations.

Carry a small bottle or perfume pendant filled with this lovely oil during the day to aid with states of anxiety, nervous tension or anger. Alternatively, make a simple room mist by pouring one cup of distilled water into a fine mist spray bottle and adding ten to twenty drops of Ylang-Ylang essential oil. Shake well before misting the room.

*"The best things are nearest:
breath in your nostrils,
light in your eyes,
flowers at your feet,
duties at your hand,
the path of God just before you."*

ROBERT LOUIS STEVENSON

*T*he following deep breathing exercises help to
fully expand the lungs, relax muscles, relieve anxiety, help
you to fall asleep, as well as to enhance vitality and youth-
fulness as more blood is pumped throughout the body.

—*Stretch the rib cage and spine (overhead arm stretches,
side to side, clasp hands in back and lift to fully open the
chest area)*

—*Inhale through the nose (count of 3) allowing the air to
be moistened, filtered and warmed.*

—*Breathe slowly in a relaxed manner with complete
exhalation (exhale count of 4)*

—*Practice breathing exercises in several positions for
varied air distribution (upper chest and abdominal,
sitting and lying down).*

Juniper Berry

Juniper communis

....

$\mathcal{A}$ famous flavor ingredient in Geneva or Holland's Gin, Juniper has also been used to purify the air in European hospitals by burning the tree's twigs and dried berries. This small evergreen tree has a wide distribution in the Northern hemisphere. It has blue-green needles and grows abundant bluish-black berries. The clear oil distilled from the crushed dried berries of this conifer tree has a penetrating pine-like aroma with a peppery overtone. Strongly antiseptic, tonic and diuretic in nature, Juniper essential oil is traditionally used for skin problems, rheumatism, water retention and colds and flu. It is warming and purifying to the body and calming and uplifting for the mind.

Juniper is a perfect essential oil for use in an electric diffuser for subtle environmental fragrancing as well as purification. In winter months when colds and flu are prevalent it can be most welcomed.

A Garden Collection of Edible Flowers:

Nasturtium, Calendula officinalis, Bachelor buttons, Violets, Roses, Borage flowers, Sweet William, Pansies, Lavatera, Bee balm, Chrysanthemums, Chamomile, Chive flowerettes, Dill, Thyme blossoms, Rosemary, Oregano, Mint, Sage, Lavender and Basil flowerettes.

Wonderful Ways with Flowers:

Toss in salads to add color and zest,
garnish appetizers for a gourmet touch,
use in herb butters to impart interesting and exotic flavors,
freeze in ice cubes for the unexpected,
decorate desserts and bake in muffins and breads,
and delight your family and friends.

Begin with patience, end with pleasure.

African Proverb, Swahili

$\mathcal{N}$ot only do plants produce life-sustaining oxygen and bring natural beauty to our living environments, but they are also living air filters. There are some plants which are especially useful for filtering air pollution and cleaning the air by consuming and digesting a multitude of chemicals and toxins.

A Collection of Clean Air Plants

Areca Palm, Arrowhead Vine, Boston Fern, Chrysanthemums, Dwarf Date Palm, English Ivy, Golden Pathos, Peace Lily, Spider plants and Striped Dracaenea.

Keep your indoor plants clean and dusted to increase their effectiveness. Be sure to include these types of plants in rooms where there are computers, fax machines and printers. In general, place 1 or 2 medium-sized plants per 100 square foot size room. Place extra plants in newly carpeted and painted rooms for additional filtering benefits.

*I*n fourth grade I made a poster with artwork and transcribed this poem on it for catechism class, and often recited it as a young girl to my father as we worked out in the strawberry patch or hayfields in New England. It is a comforting reminder that some memories, especially those associated with scent, never fade.

Out in the Fields with God

The little cares that fretted me,
I lost them yesterday,
Among the fields above the sea,
Among the winds at play,
Among the lowing of the herds,
The rustling of the trees,
Among the singing of the birds,
The humming of the bees.

The foolish fears of what might pass
I cast them all away
Among the clover-scented grass
Among the new-mown hay,
Among the hushing of the corn
Where drowsy poppies nod,
Where ill thoughts die and good are born—
Out in the fields with God.

AUTHOR UNKNOWN

If you grow fragrant old-fashioned roses, or know a neighbor who does, you will surely want to dry your own petals for the best aromatic blossoms. After they have completely dried, chop them finely using a blender or food processor.

Gentle Facial Wash

Smoothes and exfoliates the skin

1/2 cup finely ground oatmeal
1/2 cup powdered milk
2–4 Tablespoons dried Rose petals, ground (optional)
Floral water or herb tea

Use 2 teaspoons of dry mixture with enough floral water or herb tea to form a paste-like scrub. Massage gently in a circular motion over face and neck areas, avoiding the eyes. Rinse with warm water.

Beauty without virtue is like a rose without scent.

DANISH PROVERB

"Live now, believe me, wait not till tomorrow;
Gather the roses of life today."

PIERRE DE RONSARD

This herbal tea has pulled many women through stressful times … PMS, menopause and troubled relationships, and is also a favorite tea amongst friends.

Goddess Tea
An herbal infusion for women

6 parts Raspberry leaves
4 parts Chamomile flowers
2 parts Rose petals
1 part Ginger root (fresh or dried)
1 part Licorice root (ground)
1 part Rosemary herb
Honey to taste

Combine all dried ingredients in a clean glass jar and label. If using fresh ginger root, cut 1/4 inch slice per cup of tea. When using dried, 1/4 teaspoon or less to taste. To prepare, pour boiling water over 2 teaspoons herb per cup. Allow to steep for 5 minutes and strain. Enjoy hot or cold.

$\mathscr{A}$ deep-felt primeval forest scent that encourages "chi" or energy. It is made with all tree essential oils which are said to create life force energy. A powerful synergistic combination when used with the Breath of Life (breathing exercises in this book) or while practicing Chi Gong, oriental movement exercises.

Primeval Forest
An inhalation synergy of aromatic woods

1 part Scotch Pine essential oil
1 part Atlas Cedarwood essential oil
1 part Sandalwood (or Cypress) essential oil

$\mathscr{M}$ix by drops to use in an aroma lamp. Or alternatively, prepare in larger amounts to be used in an electric diffuser. This smoky-coniferous aromatic blend is excellent for general air purification, as well as a relief for sinus and lung ailments due to its cleansing effects on the respiratory system.

"You drink the scent of the woods
like water from the spring."

CHANG CHEN

Scotch Pine

Pinus sylvestris

One of over 80 species, Scotch Pine, or Norway Pine as it is commonly named, was at one time used by the American Indians to prevent scurvy. A large stately evergreen growing up to 120 feet in height, it has reddish-brown bark with grey-green needles and brown coned fruit. The best essential oil is distilled from the needles of this conifer tree yielding a clear to slightly yellow oil. Its enlivening and cooling aroma is fresh, forest-like with a dry balsamic overtone. Traditional uses include respiratory ailments, urinary tract infections and general deodorizing and air purifying benefits.

During the festive holiday season place a few drops of Scotch Pine essential oil onto pine cones and place in an open decorative bowl or tuck inside an artificial tree to enliven it with the outdoor balsam scent.

*"Healing is a matter of time,
but is sometimes also a matter of opportunity."*

HIPPOCRATES

*"This is the forest primeval.
The murmuring pines and the hemlocks …
Stand like Druids of old."*

HENRY WADSWORTH LONGFELLOW

*A*n invigorating and healthful herbal infusion that can be enjoyed hot or cold.

Refreshing Herb Tea

4 parts Lemonbalm herb
4 parts Peppermint herb
1 part ground Fennel seed
1 part freshly grated or ground Ginger root
fresh Lemon peel
Cinnamon to taste

*M*ix dried ingredients in a jar and label. To prepare bring 2 cups water to a boil. Add 2 to 3 teaspoons of herb tea, grated ginger and fresh lemon peel and simmer gently for 3 minutes. Remove from heat and strain.

Peppermint

Mentha piperita

A cross of Spearmint and Watermint, this hybrid plant, Black Mint or Brandy Mint as it is commonly called, is native to Europe. A three-foot tall herb that has serrated green aromatic leaves that are tinged purplish-brown with purple spiked flowers, it is common along stream beds and damp locations; however, it is being widely cultivated in Indiana, Oregon and Washington, USA. The partially dried flowering tops, leaves and stems are steam-distilled to yield a slightly cloudy to pale yellow-green essential oil that mellows with age. The powerful scent of peppermint oil is penetrating, sharp, grassy-mint-like and camphoraceous. It has a cooling nature and aids in clearing the head, opening the sinuses and has a general stimulating effect.

Try a drop or two on a tissue or small personal fan for a cooling breeze and inhalation remedy for lethargy, faintness, nausea or motion sickness.

$\mathcal{T}$he benefits from this simple facial steam are a well-kept secret. Facial steaming done with skin-friendly flowers and herbs is gentle, deep cleansing, detoxifying and has youth-giving advantages. After browsing through the kitchen pantry or garden, write your personal recipe on the next page and experience it for yourself.

Floral Facial Steam

1 teaspoon of the following flowers and herbs:
Calendula, Chamomile, Lavender, Elderflower,
Rose petals and Green tea herb
3 cups hot water

$\mathcal{H}$eat water and pour into a glass or ceramic bowl. Add approximately 3 teaspoons of flower mix to water and stir. With a towel, form a tent over the head, with your face about 8 inches from the water level. Keep eyes closed and steam for 15 minutes. Pat face dry and mist the face with floral water or apply your favorite moisturizer.

Every flower has its scent.

IRANIAN PROVERB

$\mathcal{T}$he following recipe is a zesty home-made family recipe. A welcomed gourmet addition to any Mediterranean or Italian dish, especially flavorful on pizza, in tomato-based sauces and homemade salad dressings.

Mediterranean Fine Herbs

A healthful aromatic herbal spice blend

4 parts Basil
2 parts of the following herbs:
Parsley, Chervil, Tarragon, and Rosemary
1 part Chives and dried chopped Garlic
Dried Onion granules and Hot Pepper flakes (optional)

$\mathcal{M}$ix the above herbs and spices and store in a spice jar. For a spicier version opt for the onion and pepper flakes for the intense flavor they lend.

Basil

Ocimum basilicum

*T*his herb's name is derived from the Greek word "basileus" for "king." A tender annual with strongly aromatic dark green ovate leaves, the distilled herb and flowering tops produce a clear to pale yellow essential oil with a light spicy and sweet, warmly balsamic aroma. This enlivening and vivifying scent is used traditionally to relieve loss of concentration, states of anxiety and mild depression. In general, it is calming to the nervous system and has an uplifting and clearing effect on the mind and emotions. In addition, it serves as an effective remedy for headaches, stress-related allergies, respiratory ailments and as a tonic for healthy gums, skin and hair growth.

Its benefits go far beyond making pesto. Basil essential oil can help anyone going through a stressful and nervous time, especially before public speaking, presentations and intense mental concentration. Inhale its scent directly from the bottle or place a few drops onto a tissue. Take a few slow deep and relaxing breaths to experience the calming and clearing effects. Definitely keep a tiny bottle in your briefcase or desk.

Do not refuse the body what it asks for.

*D*eep nocturnal slumber is critical for a healthy mind and body and largely depends on a sound nervous system. Lavender and Marjoram, among other essential oils, are said to raise serotonin levels in the body. Serotonin is a hormone produced by the brain to promote sleep as well as make you happier, calmer and less prone to illness.

Peaceful Sleep

A restful sleep synergy

7 parts Lavender essential oil
2 parts Marjoram essential oil
1 part Clary sage essential oil

*M*ix the essential oils in an amber glass bottle. Place a few drops onto bed linens or pillow. Or use a few drops in an aroma lamp or make in larger amounts to be used with an electric diffuser. Alternatively, place 20–30 drops in 4 ounces of distilled water in a fine-mist spray bottle for a natural room aromatic mister.

Lavender

Lavendula officinalis, L. angustifolia, L. vera

There are many varieties of Lavender, all of which are native to the Mediterranean, primarily France, and also to England and Yugoslavia. Common names include French Lavender, English Lavender, Garden or Common Lavender, and True Lavender. This highly aromatic two- to four-foot shrubby plant derived its name from the Latin word "lavare" which means "to wash." The Romans knew of its antiseptic effects and used it to cleanse wounds and to add to bath water. Clear to pale yellow in color, this oil is steam-distilled from the fresh flowering stalks which grow abundantly on irregular short woody stems. The botanical has grey-green leaves and violet-blue whorls of flowerettes on its broom-like spikes. Lavender oil's bouquet is floral, slightly herbal with woody overtones. Its physical and emotional effects are numerous, from first-aid treatment and skincare to stress-related disorders, such as headaches, insomnia and hypertension.

A few ways to enjoy the calming essence of Lavender: place a few drops on bed linens for a simple sleep aid; tuck lavender-scented cotton balls into drawers and closets to ward off moths and pleasantly fragrance your clothing. Place two to three drops into an aroma lamp or kettle of hot water to diffuse a subtle aroma to any room.

According to reflexology experts and Oriental medicine, certain areas on the soles of the feet correspond to other parts of the body. A good restorative foot soak and massage can affect more than just the feet. Place a handful of marbles or small round pebbles in the bottom of the foot basin to roll the feet over to massage and apply reflexology-like acu-pressure to the soles of your feet while soaking. Afterward apply a warmed vegetable oil to which you have added 2 drops of Rosemary essential oil; firmly massage each foot, giving special attention to any sore or uncomfortable areas.

Aromatic Foot Bath

4 drops Lavender essential oil
2 drops Rosemary essential oil
4 Tablespoons Sea salt or Epsom salt

Fill a basin with warm or tepid water. Mix the essential oils with the salts and add to the water. Sit in a comfortable place and allow your feet to soak for at least 15 minutes.

*"The way to health
is to have an aromatic bath
and scented massage every day."*

HIPPOCRATES

Rosemary

Rosmarinus officinalis, R. coronarium

*D*erived from the Latin "rosmarinus" meaning "sea dew," this herbaceous shrub was highly revered by the Greeks and Romans as a symbol of regeneration, strengthening the memory and honored as a sacred plant and incense. Ancient uses included it in festivals, weddings and funerals. It was popular as a strewing herb and as incense during the times of the Plague. Native to Asia, and growing abundantly in the Mediterranean region, this three-to six-foot woody aromatic perennial has dark green-silvery needle-like leaves and bluish lavender flowers. Distillation of the flowering tops and leaves yields a clear to pale yellow liquid. This warmly invigorating oil has a bracing and refreshing aroma that is woody-herbal with minty camphor overtones. Effective for general debility, aiding memory, clearing the head and respiratory system, it is as well a tonic and stimulant for the circulation and for oily skin conditions.

Try a drop or two on the side pages of a book you are reading to aid in alertness, concentration and memory attention. When studying, use the same scent consistently and again when taking an exam to enhance memory retrieval. You will be able to recall the information better due to the conditioning as well as the direct olfactory-limbic system stimulation, since memory is seated in this portion of the brain.

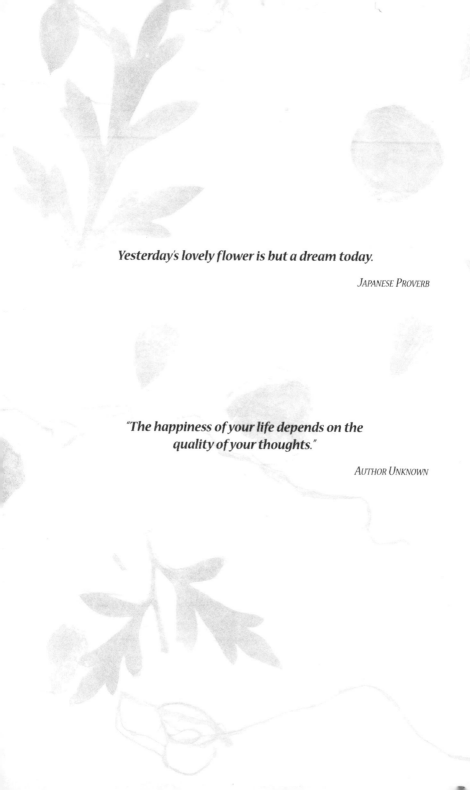

Yesterday's lovely flower is but a dream today.

JAPANESE PROVERB

*"The happiness of your life depends on the
quality of your thoughts."*

AUTHOR UNKNOWN

A delicately scented slumber-inducing sachet to tuck inside your bed pillow. These herbs and essential oils are chosen for their unique ability to induce relaxation, calm the nervous system and promote sleep. Sweet dreams…

Sweet Dreams Sleep Pillow

4 parts Sweet Woodruff herb
2 parts Lemonbalm herb
2 parts Lavender flowers
1 part each of the following:
Hops, Rose petals, Chamomile, Marjoram,
Thyme, Sage, crushed Rosemary, Southernwood,
Mugwort and Cinnamon
1 part finely grated Orris root
Lavender, Chamomile and Marjoram essential oils

*T*o make a single pillow: 1 part = 1 tablespoon. Mix the above herbs, flowers and spices in a large bowl. Add a total of 5 drops of a single essential oil or combination of the relaxing essences listed to the orris root and mix well. Add the scented orris root to the herb mixture and fill a 4" × 6" muslin sewn pillow. Sew the opening to secure the sachet contents. Tuck this sleep pillow inside your bed pillow.

Cypress

Cupressus sempervirens

*I*n Greek "sempervirens" means "lives forever" and refers to the ancient reverence for this tree as a precious medicine and purification incense. The Italian or Mediterranean Cypress is an evergreen conifer which bears round brown-grey cones. The twigs, needles and cones of this tree are steam-distilled to yield an invigorating pale yellow-green essence. Known for its refreshing and cooling effects, Cypress oil's traditional benefits include aid for respiratory ailments, especially spasmodic coughs, as well as for stress conditions like restlessness, nervous tension, irritability and PMS complaints. It is excellent for its tonic ability for oily skin, poor circulation, broken capillaries and cellulite.

Place a few drops of this purifying coniferous essential oil onto a charcoal tablet to burn as incense or try sprinkling a little on wood logs to burn in your fireplace.

"Home is where the heart is."

*H*ome can have many varying meanings to different people. Hearth, fireside, residence, birthplace, hometown or personal retreat. Common components in what makes a home are comfort, feeling cared for, and familiarity. Sights, sounds and smells help to create that haven.

"One sweetly solemn thought
Comes to me o'er and o'er;
I am nearer home today
Than I ever have been before."

PHOEBE CARY

*T*his merry-making potpourri is colorful as well as fragrant, inspiriting a feeling of warmth, abundance and welcome home.

Scented Memories

1 cup of each:
   Marjoram, Calendula flowers, Lemonbalm,
   Mint and Lavender
2 Tablespoons Rosemary herb
1 Cinnamon stick broken in pieces
1 strip Lemon peel
1/2 teaspoon Cloves
1/2 teaspoon grated Nutmeg
2 Tablespoons dried Orris root
3 drops Rose Geranium essential oil
2 drops Lemon essential oil
1 drop Peppermint essential oil

*M*ix all dried ingredients, except the orris root. In a separate bowl, mix the orris root and essential oils with the back of a spoon or mortar and pestle. Add this mixture to the potpourri. Store in a glass jar or zip-lock plastic bag to age for about a week before using.

Geranium

Pelargonium graveolens

With over 700 varieties, including many that are strictly ornamental, the Rose Geranium is a delightfully fragrant perennial shrub that grows to three feet high. Native to South Africa, this now widely cultivated botanical is primarily grown in Reunion, Egypt, Russia and China. The plant has pointed furry textured leaves with tiny pink flowers. The flowering botanical is distilled to produce a refreshing and uplifting oil that is light green to olive in color and possesses a pleasing rose-like, sweet-herbal and green efflorescence. Rose geranium oil has antibacterial and antifungal properties, making it very beneficial in skincare and throat infections. Tonic to the nervous system and regulating for female hormonal imbalances, Geranium has a traditionally wide application, from relieving depression and balancing the emotions to treatment of varicose veins and cellulite.

Rose Geranium leaves are wonderfully scented and good enough to eat. Some gourmet restaurants sugarcoat the leaves and flowers for cakes or make deliciously fragrant sorbets from their leaves. An herbal tea can easily be prepared by infusing the leaves and flowers in hot water. A pleasing sipping tisane as well as an excellent gargle for ameliorating sore throats and laryngitis.

As the garden, so the gardener.

HEBREW PROVERB

*M*ost essential oils have some antibacterial germicidal effects, yet there are some that are much more powerful in this area than others. The following essential oils have proven to be effective antibacterial and antiseptic natural alternatives for room deodorizers and disinfectants.

The Antiseptic Essences

Bergamot, Citronella, all Eucalyptus types, Juniper, Lavender, Lemon, Lemongrass, Orange, Peppermint, Petitgrain, Pine, Rosemary, Sandalwood and Tea Tree essential oils.

*T*ry this simple, but very effective, natural room deodorizer to humidify the air as it purifies. Use in the kitchen, laundry room, bathroom and automobile.

Pure for Sure Spray

8 ounces distilled water
20 drops Lavender essential oil
12 drops Eucalyptus essential oil
12 drops Pine essential oil

*I*n an 8 ounce plastic fine-mist spray bottle, add the distilled water and essential oils. Label contents with directions for use. Shake well before each use, since essential oils and water do not mix.

Eucalyptus

Eucalyptus globulus, E. radiata,
E. polybractea, E. smithii, E. dives, E. citriodora

There are over 700 different species of Eucalyptus with many widely varying essential oil characteristics and aromas. The best known variety is Eucalyptus globulus, or Blue Gum or Fever Tree. The Eucalyptus is a fast growing tree reaching 300 to 400 feet in height, natively growing in Australia, North and South Africa, India and Southern Europe. It has smooth grey bark with leathery leaves. The essential oil, which is clear and eventually yellows with age, is produced by steam distillation of the fresh or partially dried leaves and twigs. The oil has a sharp woody-sweet and camphoraceous scent reminiscent of chest cold medicine. This purifying, slightly cooling essence is highly antiseptic and antiviral—easily opening the sinuses and respiratory passages and clearing the head.

When experiencing the aroma of Eucalyptus, you may be transported back to your childhood days and memories of staying home from school, vapor steams and chest rubs when you had a cold. Eucalyptus has been used for generations as a remedial treatment for colds and flu and the congestion which is associated with respiratory ailments.

Bergamot

Citrus bergamia

$\mathcal{N}$amed after a small town in Southern Italy, this small pear-shaped fruit is best known for giving Earl Grey tea its unique flavor. The greenish yellow fruit peels are expressed to produce a pale lime colored essential oil which later turns shades of olive. Grown on small evergreen trees, the fruit yields a delicate spice-like citrus aroma with a balsamic undertone. This refreshing essential oil is used traditionally for stress-related conditions such as anxiety, nervous tension, PMS, depression and appetite disorders. Antiseptic in nature, the oil is a natural deodorant and is applied in a variety of skin problems, mouth infections and inflammatory conditions such as tonsillitis, bronchitis, cystitis, intestinal colic and hemorrhoids.

Bergamot aids in creating equilibrium or homeostasis on both the emotional and physical levels and may be helpful in treating addictions and underlying stress conditions. Try diffusing the essential oil of Bergamot in home or workplace and note your personal experiences and reactions to this satisfying citrus-like mood balancer.

*"Is it possible that I am so busy doing
that I no longer have time to enjoy being?"*

WILSON

Relax . . .
Swing
Rock in a rocking chair
Lounge in a hammock
Watch the clouds
Sip herb tea
or create your own restful repose.

*"Though nothing can bring back the hour
Of splendor in the grass, of glory in the flower."*

WILLIAM WORDSWORTH

Along the way take time to smell the flowers …

*P*lace a drop or two of essential oil to a hand-held fan or folded newspaper to soothe your mind with a delicate breeze. Use a drop of Peppermint to cool, Lemon to refresh and brighten the day or Sweet Mandarin to bring back childhood memories.

"O World, I cannot hold thee close enough!"

EDNA ST. VINCENT MILLAY

Mandarin

Citrus reticulata, C. nobilis, C. madurensis

Mandarin, also known as Tangerine or Satsuma, is the name given to the citrus fruit native to Southern China where it was traditionally given as a token of respect to the Mandarins (majesties) of that country. An evergreen tree, which can reach twenty feet in height, has shiny green leaves and fragrant white flowers. The orange-like fruit has loose skin, which is expressed to yield a yellowish-orange oil. The Mandarin essence has a sweet delicate orange-like aroma with tangy-floral overtones. Antiseptic in nature, the oil is more commonly used for its stress-relieving benefits for insomnia, mental fatigue, nervous tension and overactivity. A sunny emanating scent favored by children and children-at-heart.

Add one drop of Mandarin essential oil to a tablespoon of warm vegetable oil, such as safflower or canola. Use this delicately aromatic massage oil to relax a child in the evening. Younger children will enjoy having their feet massaged while older children will appreciate a hand massage. Note: This oil preparation is not meant to be used on babies or toddlers who may rub their eyes or suck on their hands.

When one pours out his heart, he feels lighter.

YIDDISH PROVERB

*What soap is for the body,
tears are for the soul.*

JEWISH PROVERB

*T*he recipe to follow is a nurturing bath when there are feelings of sadness and grief, loss and mild depression due to anger. Talk to a friend to lighten your heart, and care for yourself gently by taking a long warm reassuring bath when you can. Soak for as long as you need to.

Aromatic Bath for Melancholy

1/4 cup honey
3 drops Lavender essential oil
3 drops Ylang ylang essential oil
2 drops Basil essential oil
2 drops Rose Geranium essential oil
1 drop Grapefruit essential oil

*M*ix the essential oils in the honey. Draw a warm bath and add the aromatic honey after it has filled.

Grapefruit

Citrus paradisii

A citrus native to tropical Asia, this hybrid is believed to have come from C. grandi and C. sinesis. Widely cultivated in California and Florida, USA, the Grapefruit is a tree with glossy leaves, fragrant white flowers and abundant large yellow fruits. The fruit peels yield a pale yellow oil from expression with highly antiseptic and astringent properties. The scent is very bright, sweet-citrus and most refreshing. This oil is known for its antidepressant, anti-stress and energizing euphoric-like properties. It has a deeply cleansing effect on obese, sluggish and congested skin types.

Do you cut your grapefruit to eat the fruit?

Did you realize you were missing out on a sparkling citrus olfactory adventure?

Peel your grapefruit instead, because tearing open the thick rind will release tiny bursts of essential oil from its fruit. A truly revitalizing morning meal.

The essential oils that are utilized to encourage Hope are:

Bergamot, **Clary sage**, **Lavender**, **Bulgarian Rose**, **Rose Geranium**, **Grapefruit**, **Sweet Orange**, **Lemon**, **Ylang ylang**, **Sandalwood and Neroli.**

Hope is sovereign balsam.

AMERICAN PROVERB

"When the rosebud ripened to the rose,
In both I read thy name."

RALPH WALDO EMERSON

The synergistic combination of essential oils derived from fruits is a citrus-fresh reminder of summer and joyful times. Use in aroma lamp, diffuser or mixed with distilled water for a room fragrance.

Tropical Oasis

3 parts Mandarin essential oil
3 parts Lemon essential oil
2 parts Lemongrass essential oil
2 parts Grapefruit essential oil
2 parts Bergamot essential oil

Hope without work is like a tree without fruit.

LEBANESE PROVERB

Lemongrass

Cymbopogon citratus

Also known as East Indian Verbena, this aromatic perennial grass is native to India but grows in many tropical areas. It is fast growing, reaching two and half feet before it is cut, partially dried and steam distilled. Lemongrass oil is slightly yellow in color with a strong lemon-like scent with green overtones. It is slightly cooling, fresh and vivifying. Lemongrass essential oil is known to invigorate the body and energize the mind, making it useful for stress conditions, mental fatigue and general debility. Also, this essence has traditional benefits as an insecticide, fungicide and antiseptic agent.

Try adding ten to twenty drops to a pump bottle of your favorite liquid hand soap to refresh as well as naturally fight germs.

"A friend is someone who takes action for another's good."

AUTHOR UNKNOWN

Ointment and perfume rejoice the heart;
so doth the sweetness of a man's friend by hearty counsel.

PROVERBS 27 : 9

A floral-sweet heavenly scent that is extremely pleasurable, this synergistic blend is euphoric, anti-depressant, regulating and balancing on the emotions and mental state. Use this aromatherapy recipe along with journal writing and share your feelings with a close friend.

Nature's Answer

A synergy for mild depression

4 parts Clary sage essential oil
4 parts Ylang ylang essential oil
3 parts Rose Geranium essential oil
2 parts Basil essential oil
1 part Sandalwood (or Frankincense) essential oil

*M*ix the above essential oils in an amber glass bottle and label. Place 3 or 4 drops in an aroma lamp or larger amount for an electric diffuser, for inhalation use. Alternatively, place a drop or two on a tissue or within a perfume pendant for personal use.

Sandalwood

Santalum album

*C*ommonly named East Indian Sandalwood or Mysore Sandalwood, this tree was once a popular wood to construct temples, prepare exotic incense, for ancient perfumes and for cosmetic preparations. Native to tropical Asia, this evergreen tree grows on the roots of other (host) trees for almost seven years until the host tree dies. Upon maturity, which can take upwards of 30 years, the Sandalwood tree can reach forty feet tall. It has leathery leaves and small mauve colored flowers. The essential oil is produced from the mature heartwood and roots of this vanishing species, after it has been felled, ground, powdered and dried. Its precious oil bears a softly-sweet balsamic aroma that is exotic, woody and rich. It is known traditionally as a calming anti-depressant and aphrodisiac, but is also useful for genito-urinary tract infections and inflammations because of its antiseptic, antifungal and tonic nature.

Due to the near extinction of this tree, it is best to use other essential oil alternatives for particular aromatherapy treatments to lower the demand for this heartwood essence and protect the Santalum species. Preservation of the earth's natural resources must take precedence if we are to be privileged in utilizing its precious gifts for human health and enjoyment.

Not that which is beautiful
but that which pleases is beautiful.

YIDDISH PROVERB

Beauty is but a blossom.

ENGLISH PROVERB

"Never a day passes
but that I do myself the honor
to commune with some of nature's varied forms."

GEORGE WASHINGTON CARVER

$\mathcal{U}$ntil recently, the sense of smell has been under-rated and practically ignored by mainstream scientific and health researchers. We use our olfactory sense to fully enjoy and literally take in life's pleasures, as well as to warn us of danger, such as in the case of food poisoning, fire, gas intoxication etc. Many people who have lost their ability to smell often have a higher incidence of depression, weight gain, a decreased interest in sex, and are at greater risk for accidents. It is hard to realize how important our sense of smell really is because it's impossible to imagine life without it!

Healthy Olfaction

Suggestions for stimulating your sense of smell

Avoid cigarette and cigar smoke

Remove chemical cleaners and pollutants from your living and working spaces

Purify your environment using the Clean Air Plants and only natural essential oils to fragrance

Eat more Lecithin-rich foods and fresh fish

See your doctor regarding the possibility of a nutritional deficiency

Inquire about the side-effects of the medications you are taking

Myrrh

Commiphora myrrha

 or at least 4000 years Myrrh has been used for
incense in religious ceremonies, embalming purposes, as a
disinfectant in battle fields, and as an anointment for
kings. It was a primary ingredient in the Holy Oil of the
Jews and Kyphi of the Egyptians. Hippocrates mentioned
Myrrh in more than fifty medical prescriptions, believing
it had the exceptional ability to treat wounds and skin
sores. A small tree that stands nine feet tall, Myrrh is
native to the Middle East. Its gnarled thorny branches
bear aromatic trifoliate leaves. Through natural fissures
in the bark, or when the tree is incised, a pale yellow oleo-
resin exudes and later hardens into reddish-brown colored "tears" that are quite brittle and have a powdery looking surface. The essential oil is produced by steam distillation of the oleo-resin of these tears. The oil is viscous and
red-amber in color. It has a restorative aroma which is
deep, smoky, balsamic and slightly bitter. Traditional uses
are for protective, anti-aging skincare, for dry skin conditions where there is cracking, for mouth ulcers and fungal
infections. It is also the ancient element in incense and
perfume.

*H*ave you taken a few moments to listen to your thoughts today? Did you take good care of yourself? Sit and be quiet, close your eyes and look inward. Release the tension and breathe slowly, deeply and fully. When you are ready, write down your innermost thoughts, your unfulfilled desires and dreams. Remember to honor who you are and why you are here. You are special. There is only one you in the entire universe, and never again will there be anyone exactly like you!

With all your knowledge know thyself.

ENGLISH PROVERB

*"That which is grows,
while that which is not becomes."*

GALEN

*"Just do what you love and believe
and it will come naturally."*

AUTHOR UNKNOWN

*"Our doing brings success,
but our being bears fruit.
The great paradox of our lives
is that we are often concerned
about what we do or still can do,
but we are most likely to be remembered
for who we were."*

HENRI J. M. NOUWEN

Atlas Cedarwood

Cedrus atlantica

Native to the Atlas mountains in Algeria, this tree is known as African Cedar. A magnificent pyramid-shaped evergreen tree which grows over 120 feet high, its strongly aromatic hard wood, roots and saw dust is distilled to yield a camphorous liquid which varies in color from yellow to deep amber-orange. The aroma is warm, balsamic with a slight sweet-tenacious dry afternote. Traditional applications include a multitude of benefits to combat skin infections and respiratory ailments such as bronchitis. It is also an excellent air purifier, insect repellent and fungicide. Effective for nervous states, specifically anxiety, anger and fear, this ancient oil has been used most for meditation and ceremonial purposes.

Closets, drawers, hangers and hope chests were commonly constructed from Cedarwood to deter moths and other insects from infesting woolen clothing, fine linens and blankets. Alternatively, you can purchase doweling or blocks of less expensive wood and place several drops of Cedarwood essential oil on them to be absorbed. Tuck in closets, sock drawers and storage areas to obtain the same benefits.

A purely rich, exotic odorous blend reserved for special occasions due to the costly attars and essences it contains. This is genuinely an amorous blend.

Love in a Mist
An aphrodisiac and euphoric synergy

10 drops Ylang ylang essential oil
3 drops Clary Sage essential oil
2 drops Patchouli essential oil
2 drops Black Pepper essential oil
2 drops Neroli essential oil
1 drop Bulgarian Rose essential oil
1 drop Jasmine absolute

*C*ombine the essential oils in a small bottle. To use place 3 to 5 drops of the oils into an aroma lamp or potpourri burner, using the lesser amount for a small room.

Love is a flower
which turns into fruit
at marriage.

FINNISH PROVERB

Neroli

Citrus aurantium

*B*elieved to be named after the Italian princess Anne-Marie of Nerola, who favored the luxurious scent of this fragrance for her personal garments and toiletries. Native to China, the Sweet orange tree grows to 30 feet and produces small white fragrant blossoms used to dis-till or solvent-extract the delicate oil of Neroli. The oil is pale yellow and possesses a divine slightly citrus-floral sweetness that is tranquilizing and peaceful. Traditionally honored for its neuro-tonic, antidepressant and sedative effects, Neroli is useful as a hypnotic and sleep aid, as well as for troubled skin, poor circulation and PMS complaints.

Neroli is sadly often adulterated with cheaper chemi-cals and fragrance materials because the true essence is very expensive. An alternative to enjoying this odorous sensation is to grow a small orange tree in your home. Just a few flowers in bloom is all it takes to fill a small room with luxurious perfume.

*To be for one day entirely at leisure
is to be for one day immortal.*

CHINESE PROVERB

When the well is full it will run over.

ENGLISH PROVERB

Design your own personal spa:

*G*ather all your pampering bath paraphernalia such as bath pillow, cool eye gel pack (or cold tea bags), loofahs and sea sponges, big fluffy absorbent towels and bath robe, bath toys, aromatherapy candles, floral water to mist your face, and a soothing herb tea to sip as you soak. Wrap your hair in an oil treatment while you are in the tub, or envelop yourself in a mud wrap or face mask. Create privacy with a "Do Not Disturb" sign at the bathroom door. Put on your favorite relaxing music, nature soundtrack or appreciate the solitude of silence. You will experience the opulence and abundance of taking extra special care of your body and soul. Life is sweet.

Indulgent Milk Bath

$1/2$–1 cup heavy cream (or half milk and cream)
4 drops Ylang ylang essential oil
4 drops Lavender essential oil
2 drops Patchouli essential oil
1 drop Bulgarian Rose essential oil (optional)
a handful of fresh clean rose petals to float in water (optional)

*I*n a bowl or cup combine the cream with the essential oils. Draw a warm bath. Add to the bath after it has filled.

Patchouli

Pogostemon patchouli, P. cablin

An herbaceous three-foot tall perennial shrub, native to tropical Asia, with soft furry ovate leaves and white flowers tinged with purple. The essential oil is steam-distilled from the dried young aromatic leaves. The essence is dark amber-brown and has a thick viscosity. Its haunting aroma becomes softer, sweeter and less tenacious with age, yielding a smoky-sweet, rich and earthy fragrance. Well known for its aphrodisiac and antidepressant qualities, Patchouli is also useful as an immune stimulant, antifungal agent and anti-inflammatory treatment for skin problems.

The fragrance of Patchouli has made a comeback from the 1960s. That may be good news for some and perhaps bad memories for others. Are there any memories this earthy scent conjures up for you? Write down your recollections here. There are sometimes powerfully strong associations between scent and memory.

"It is safe to look within.
Each time you look deeper into yourself,
you are going to find incredibly beautiful treasures within you!"

LOUISE L. HAY

"For what the centre brings
must obviously be
that which remains to the end
And was there from eternity."

GOETHE

*T*he perfect weight of the pillow makes it ever so soothing and the lavender scent is tranquilizing. Keep at the bedside or at the office for relaxing comfort during times of stress, tension headaches or eye strain. Heat the pillow by microwaving for about one minute and it will provide penetrating comfort to sore muscles and joints. Simply lie down, and place the pillow across closed eyes.

Comforting Eye Pillow

1 cup Flax seed
1 cup Lavender flowers
3-5 drops Lavender essential oil

*M*ix the Lavender flowers and Flax seed in a bowl. Sprinkle the essential oils in the mixture and combine well with a spoon. Fill a 4″ × 8″ satin or silk sewn pillow with the herb-seed mix and sew the opening.

The flowers that keep
Their odor to themselves all day;
But when the sunlight dies away,
Let the delicious secret out
To every breeze that roams about.

ANONYMOUS

When cultivating your Evening Garden's perfume-scape:

*P*lant your night bloomers close to sitting areas and walk ways. Include the silvery foliage and white flowered botanicals in your design so you can enjoy the moonlight's reflection in their luminous colors.

An Evening Garden Collection

Soapwort (Saponaria officinalis), Sweet Rocket (Hesperis matronalis), Evening Primrose (Oenthera odorata), Night-scented Stock (Matthiola longipetula), Four O' Clocks (Mirabilis jalapa), Garden Phlox (Phlox paniculata), Night-Blooming Jasmine (Jasminum officinale) and Flowering Tobacco (Nicotiana alata).

Use only unscented candles in your garden so you will not distract from their subtle nocturnal emanation.

Drape fine netting over a settee for protection against pests.

Even a small star shines in the darkness.

FINNISH PROVERB

Tea Tree

Melaleuca alternifolia

$\mathcal{N}$ative to Australia, where it has a long historical use among the Aborigines as an herbal tea, this small narrow-leaved paperbark tree grows to twenty feet in height. It has needle-like leaves with bottlebrush-like flowers ranging in color from yellow to purple. A camphoraceous oil is produced by distillation of the tree leaves and twigs to yield a clear to pale yellowish-green liquid. The highly antibacterial, antifungal and antiviral oil has a sharp, spicy-medicinal and eucalyptus-like aroma. Benefits of this oil are far reaching: from a powerful immune stimulant and anti-infectious agent to first-aid treatment. It is also useful for various skin and nail problems, respiratory infections and fungal afflictions.

Gentle to use directly on skin irritations, insect bites and most minor skin infections. Dab a drop or two onto the affected area or mix with a natural ointment for a multi-beneficial first-aid treatment.

References:

     Every effort has been made to give credit to the authors of the references printed in this book. However, my sources have been many and varied, as I have collected them for many years, gathering from books, magazine articles and note cards, as well as from family and friends. Should an error be noted, please write to the Publisher and it will be corrected with the next printing.

Bartlett, John, *Bartlett's Familiar Quotations*, Sixteenth Edition, Little, Brown and Company, 1992.

Cornell, Joseph, *Listening to Nature*, Dawn Publications, USA 1987.

Gibran, Kahlil, *The Prophet*, Alfred A. Knopf Inc., NY 1980.

Hay, Louise L., *Heart Thoughts*, Hay House Inc., 1990.

Kipling, Rudyard, *Rudyard Kipling Complete Verse*, Definitive Edition, Double Day, 1940.

Mieder, Wolfgang, *The Prentice Hall Encyclopedia of World Proverbs*, MJF Books, 1986.

Minter, Sue, *The Healing Garden*, Headline Book Publishing, 1994.

Nouwen, Henri J.M., *Our Greatest Gift*, Harper Collins Publisher, 1985.

Shakespeare, William, *Shakespeare Complete Works*, Oxford University Press, 1984.

Walker, Alice, *In Search of Our Mother's Gardens*, Harcourt Brace Jovanovich Publishing, 1983.

_____, *New Oxford Book of American Verse*, Oxford University Press, 1976.

_____, *Poems: Selections from the Golden Treasury of Poetry*, Golden Press, NY, 1968.

_____, *Songs of the Earth*, Running Press, 1995.

_____, *Sisters*, Heartland Samplers, Inc., 1992.

"When the heart speaks, take good notes."

Notes